To Kate Pollard

TAURUS

A guide to living your best astrological life

STELLA ANDROMEDA

ILLUSTRATED BY EVI O. STUDIO

Hardie Grant

BOOKS

Introduction   7

I.

Get to Know Taurus

Taurus characteristics   31
Physical Taurus   34
How Taurus communicates   37
Taurus careers   38
How Taurus chimes   41
Who loves whom?   44

II.

The Taurus Deep Dive

The Taurus home   55
Self-care   57
Food and cooking   59
How Taurus handles money   61
How Taurus handles the boss   62
What is Taurus like to live with?   65
How to handle a break-up   66
How Taurus wants to be loved   69
Taurus' sex life   72

III.

Give Me More

Your birth chart   76
The Moon effect   80
The 10 planets   83
The four elements   89
Cardinal, fixed and mutable signs   92
The 12 houses   95
The ascendant   101
Saturn return   103
Mercury retrograde   104

Further reading   108
Acknowledgements   109
About the author   111

Introduction

Inscribed on the forecourt of the ancient Greek temple of Apollo at Delphi are the words 'know thyself'. This is one of the 147 Delphic maxims, or rules to live by, attributed to Apollo himself, and was later extended by the philosopher Socrates to the sentence, 'The unexamined life is not worth living.'

People seek a variety of ways of knowing themselves, of coming to terms with life and trying to find ways to understand the challenges of human existence, often through therapy or belief systems like organised religion. These are ways in which we strive to understand the relationships we have with ourselves and others better, seeking out particular tools that enable us to do so.

As far as systems of understanding human nature and experience go, astrology has much to offer through its symbolic use of the constellations of the heavens, the depictions of the zodiac signs, the planets and their energetic effects. Many people find accessing this information and harnessing its potential a useful way of thinking about how to manage their lives more effectively.

What is astrology?

In simple terms, astrology is the study and interpretation of how the planets can influence us, and the world in which we live, through an understanding of their positions at a specific place in time. The practice of astrology relies on a combination of factual knowledge of the characteristics of these positions and their psychological interpretation.

Astrology is less of a belief system and more of a tool for living, from which ancient and established wisdom can be drawn. Any of us can learn to use astrology, not so much for divination or telling the future, but as a guidebook that provides greater insight and a more thoughtful way of approaching life. Timing is very much at the heart of astrology, and knowledge of planetary configurations and their relationship to each other at specific moments in time can assist in helping us with the timing of some of our life choices and decisions.

Knowing when major life shifts can occur – because of particular planetary configurations such as a Saturn return (see page 103) or Mercury retrograde (see page 104) – or what it means to have Venus in your seventh house (see pages 85 and 98), while recognising the specific characteristics of your sign, are all tools that you can use to your advantage. Knowledge is power, and astrology can be a very powerful supplement to approaching life's ups and downs and any relationships we form along the way.

The 12 signs of the zodiac

Each sign of the zodiac has a range of recognisable characteristics, shared by people born under that sign. This is your Sun sign, which you probably already know – and the usual starting point from which we each begin to explore our own astrological paths. Sun sign characteristics can be strongly exhibited in an individual's make-up; however, this is only part of the picture.

Usually, how we appear to others is tempered by the influence of other factors – and these are worth bearing in mind. Your ascendant sign is equally important, as is the positioning of your Moon. You can also look to your opposite sign to see what your Sun sign may need a little more of, to balance its characteristics.

After getting to know your Sun sign in the first part of this book, you might want to dive into the Give Me More section (see pages 74–105) to start to explore all the particulars of your birth chart. These will give you far greater insight into the myriad astrological influences that may play out in your life.

Sun signs

It takes 365 (and a quarter, to be precise) days for the Earth to orbit the Sun and in so doing, the Sun appears to us to spend a month travelling through each sign of the zodiac. Your Sun sign is therefore an indication of the sign that the Sun was travelling through at the time of your birth. Knowing what Sun signs you and your family, friends and lovers are provides you with just the beginning of the insights into character and personality that astrology can help you discover.

On the cusp

For those for whom a birthday falls close to the end of one Sun sign and the beginning of another, it's worth knowing what time you were born. There's no such thing, astrologically, as being 'on the cusp' – because the signs begin at a specific time on a specific date, although this can vary a little year on year. If you are not sure, you'll need to know your birth date, birth time and birth place to work out accurately to which Sun sign you belong. Once you have these, you can consult an astrologer or run your details through an online astrology site program (see page 108) to give you the most accurate birth chart possible.

Taurus

The bull

✱

21 APRIL–20 MAY

Grounded, sensual and appreciative
of bodily pleasures, Taurus is a fixed
earth sign endowed by its ruling
planet Venus with grace and a love
of beauty, despite its depiction
as a bull. Generally characterised
by an easy and uncomplicated, if
occasionally stubborn, approach to
life, Taurus' opposite sign is
watery Scorpio.

Aries

The ram

✱

21 MARCH–20 APRIL

Astrologically the first sign of the
zodiac, Aries appears alongside the
vernal (or spring) equinox. A cardinal
fire sign, depicted by the ram, it is
the sign of beginnings and ruled
by planet Mars, which represents a
dynamic ability to meet challenges
energetically and creatively. Its
opposite sign is airy Libra.

Gemini

The twins

★

21 MAY–20 JUNE

A mutable air sign symbolised by the twins, Gemini tends to see both sides of an argument, its speedy intellect influenced by its ruling planet Mercury. Tending to fight shy of commitment, this sign also epitomises a certain youthfulness of attitude. Its opposite sign is fiery Sagittarius.

Cancer

The crab

★

21 JUNE–21 JULY

Depicted by the crab and the tenacity of its claws, Cancer is a cardinal water sign, emotional and intuitive, its sensitivity protected by its shell. Ruled by the maternal Moon, the shell also represents the security of home, to which Cancer is committed. Its opposite sign is earthy Capricorn.

Leo

The lion

★

22 JULY–21 AUGUST

A fixed fire sign, ruled by the Sun, Leo loves to shine and is an idealist at heart, positive and generous to a fault. Depicted by the lion, Leo can roar with pride and be confident and uncompromising, with a great faith and trust in humanity. Its opposite sign is airy Aquarius.

Virgo

The virgin

★

22 AUGUST–21 SEPTEMBER

Traditionally represented as a maiden or virgin, this mutable earth sign is observant, detail oriented and tends towards self-sufficiency. Ruled by Mercury, Virgos benefit from a sharp intellect that can be self-critical, while often being very health conscious. Its opposite sign is watery Pisces.

Scorpio

The scorpion

★

22 OCTOBER–21 NOVEMBER

Given to intense feelings, as
befits a fixed water sign, Scorpio
is depicted by the scorpion – linking
it to the rebirth that follows death –
and is ruled by both Pluto and Mars.
With a strong spirituality and deep
emotions, Scorpio needs security to
transform its strength. Its opposite
sign is earthy Taurus.

Libra

The scales

★

22 SEPTEMBER–21 OCTOBER

A cardinal air sign, ruled by Venus,
Libra is all about beauty, balance
(as depicted by the scales) and
harmony in its rather romanticised,
ideal world. With a strong aesthetic
sense, Libra can be both arty and
crafty, but also likes fairness and
can be very diplomatic. Its
opposite sign is fiery Aries.

Sagittarius

The archer

✳

22 NOVEMBER–21 DECEMBER

Depicted by the archer, Sagittarius is a mutable fire sign that's all about travel and adventure, in body or mind, and is very direct in approach. Ruled by the benevolent Jupiter, Sagittarius is optimistic with lots of ideas; liking a free rein, but with a tendency to generalise. Its opposite sign is airy Gemini.

Capricorn

The goat

✳

22 DECEMBER–20 JANUARY

Ruled by Saturn, Capricorn is a cardinal earth sign associated with hard work and depicted by the sure-footed and sometimes playful goat. Trustworthy and unafraid of commitment, Capricorn is often very self-sufficient and has the discipline for the freelance working life. Its opposite sign is the watery Cancer.

Aquarius

The water carrier

★

21 JANUARY–19 FEBRUARY

Confusingly, given its depiction by the water carrier, Aquarius is a fixed air sign ruled by the unpredictable Uranus, sweeping away old ideas with innovative thinking. Tolerant, open-minded and all about humanity, its vision is social with a conscience. Its opposite sign is fiery Leo.

Pisces

The fish

★

20 FEBRUARY–20 MARCH

Acutely responsive to its surroundings, Pisces is a mutable water sign depicted by two fish, swimming in opposite directions, sometimes confusing fantasy with reality. Ruled by Neptune, its world is fluid, imaginative and empathetic, often picking up on the moods of others. Its opposite sign is earthy Virgo.

Know

Taurus

The sign the Sun
was travelling in at the
time you were born is the
ultimate starting point
in exploring your character
and personality through
the zodiac.

YOUR SUN SIGN

Fixed earth sign,
depicted by the bull.

Ruled by Venus,
the planet associated with
the Roman goddess of beauty,
fertility, prosperity and love.

OPPOSITE SIGN

Scorpio

STATEMENT OF SELF

'I have.'

Lucky colour

Green, including the blue-greens of the turquoise spectrum, resonate with the gentility and refinement of the sign ruled by Venus. Wear these colours and connect with your Taurus energy when you need a psychological boost and additional courage, choosing accessories – shoes, gloves, socks, hat, or even underwear – if you don't have other clothes in this colour.

Lucky day

Friday. The end of the working week for most of us,
when the hard-working bull can look forward to some rest.
Friday actually links the Old English goddess Frigg with
her Roman counterpart, Venus, and we also see this in
the French word for Friday, *Vendredi.*

Lucky gem

Emerald. The traditional green of the emerald reminds us that Taurus is an earth sign, and the flashing green fire of this precious stone is also thought to protect Taurus from green-eyed jealousy.

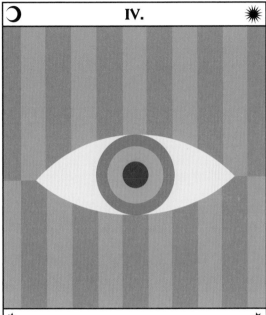

Locations

Taurus countries include Australia, Ireland, Tanzania and Switzerland, all of which are considered astrologically beneficial to those born under this sign; while cities ruled by Taurus include Honolulu, Dublin, Lucerne and Palermo.

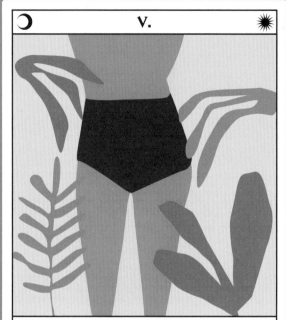

Holidays

Taurus likes to connect with the more sensual qualities of the earth and loves luxury, so holidays in beautiful locations that connect them to their bodies – like a spa destination in Thailand or an upmarket yoga retreat in the forests of Montana – may be an option. Taurus also loves food, so you may find them on a gourmet city break to sample new cuisines, in anywhere from Italy to Indonesia.

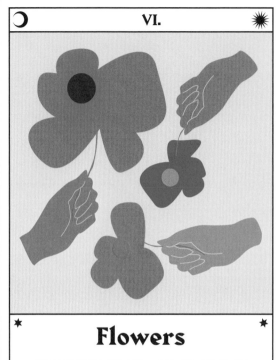

Flowers

The poppy is one of two flowers considered lucky for
this Sun sign. The other is the indomitable, sweet-scented
violet. Both help reinforce the power of Taurus.

Trees

The ash, cypress and apple tree are all associated with Taurus. The apple tree in particular, is associated with the goddess of love, and symbolises a connection to the earth.

VIII.

Pets

The sensual stroking of a cat is a very Taurean pleasure,
while a long-haired breed that needs grooming, like
a Persian cat, will give additional joy.

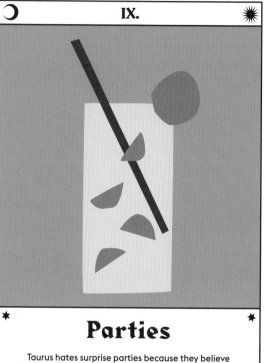

★ ★

Parties

Taurus hates surprise parties because they believe
they know better than anyone how to create a beautiful
event. A candlelit dinner for 30, with a 12-course *degustation*
menu would be their ideal celebration. Grapefruit juice and
Prosecco will get the party going, while a Chartreuse mojito
has all the ingredients to charm the most bullish of guests.

★ ★

Taurus characteristics

The key words for those born under Taurus are dependable, tenacious and hard-working. Sometimes depicted as the strong, silent type, this may sound rather boring, but this solid reliability is like a prize fertile bull balanced by a practical and compassionate nature: Taurus in earth mother mode will be the one turning up with a meal for that sick friend.

For Taurus, their security lies mainly in material possessions and they are not suited to a nomadic existence, preferring to put down roots and create a stable home life, wherever they are. This need for security means that Taurus is often good with money, making it and keeping it and often spending it on their home, creating a secure place for themselves and their beautiful purchases. Taurus likes to feel contained and is very self-contained in many ways, to the point of appearing reserved and keeping their feelings private. And because of a desire for permanence and a dislike of change, Taurus tends to be averse to risk, preferring definite outcomes based on known factors rather than backing a hunch or acting on a whim.

Ruled by Venus, planet of beauty and harmony, with an instinct for colour and design, Taurus has a natural flair for creating beautiful things but, being a practical sign, they like to translate this into something solid and enduring. Think of the Spanish artist Joan Miró, with his hands-on abstract paintings, collages, sculptures and tapestries. He is typical of a Taurus. If they are not creating something themselves, then their keen eye for both beauty and a bargain often makes them good art collectors and dealers. Taurus' sensual tastes also run to food and wine, with a deep appreciation of gourmet cooking and indulgence. Delicious food is always on the menu and many Taureans are happy to spend long hours in the kitchen creating a feast.

Considered one of the least complicated of the Sun signs, Taurus is an intriguing mix of earthiness and elegance. But being a fixed sign, Taureans don't much like change, and aren't particularly inclined to spontaneity either: not for them the last-minute dash to the airport with just a toothbrush in their pocket. They'll be the ones at the First Class check-in desk with the matching Louis Vuitton luggage. For them, abrupt changes of plan can be alarming and it's at this point that the bull can dig in its heels and paw the ground, provoking all that famous Taurean stubbornness in response. This is the Taurus downside: they can be dogmatic, resistant to change and secretive. Generally slow to anger, Taurus is no pushover and can explode if pushed too far.

TEMPERING
THE EARTH

The key characteristics of any
Sun sign can be balanced out
(or sometimes reinforced) by the
characteristics of other signs in the
same birth chart, particularly those
of the ascendant and the Moon.
So if someone doesn't appear to
be typical of their Sun sign, that's
why. However, those nascent Taurus
aspects will always be there as
a key influence, informing an
individual's approach to life.

Physical
Taurus

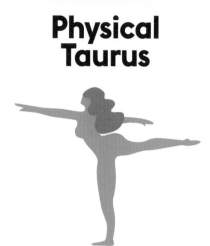

Usually strong-looking in features and build and with a direct gaze, the grounded and physically confident Taurus has a solid but graceful energy, keeping them centred and capable of being a very still, calm and reassuring presence. Because their sensual appetites also run to an enjoyment of food, they may carry some surplus body weight, but this tends to enhance a sense of powerful masculinity in men and a soft femininity in women, which is very attractive.

Health

Taurus rules the throat, home of the Adam's apple (the apple tree is their tree), and while they may have beautiful speaking and singing voices as a consequence, this is also an area of vulnerability. Inclined to sore throats and problems with the larynx and vocal chords, their voice can also express both their pleasure and their anxiety. They may too be susceptible to problems with the thyroid gland, also situated in the throat. Abstemious health fads don't cut much ice with the sensual nature of Taurus, but their love of beauty may extend to personal vanity, so keeping an eye on their calorie count may be a feature of this.

Exercise

Gyms tend to bore Taurus, but focusing on their bodies in yoga can be helpful, as can swimming. There is a tendency to embark on short-lived exercise regimes that all too often end up feeling incompatible with the bull's luxurious way of life. They often like to walk or even to run, partly to get to their destination quicker. Factoring a walk into every day is a good way for Taurus to exercise.

How Taurus communicates

Often blessed with a beautiful voice, Taurus can beguile you with carefully thought-out words, while their open body language makes them appear very approachable. Don't, however, expect any particularly light-hearted repartee or much in the way of flirtation. When they speak, they generally say what they mean and mean what they say. Warm and empathetic, Taurus is by nature a good listener, but they don't always answer straight away; and often only when they're sure of what they want to say. Their approach to problem-solving is to consider things for a while and then make suggestions that are sensible and practical. When it comes to sharing their own problems, Taurus tends to take their time with this, too, and will seldom display feelings openly.

Taurus careers

You'll find many Taurus types opt for careers that are very 'hands on': careers in the kitchen, garden, or in the hair and make-up department. Happy to get their hands dirty, many Taureans are skilled gardeners, and enjoy growing to eat even if this is only herbs in a window pot. A combination of design for practical purposes is also attractive to Taurus and this can extend from working in construction to architecture, or other industries where design and a love of beauty and order have a tangible outcome. With their acumen in money matters, a career in financial services can also reap big rewards.

Less cerebral than their airy counterparts, Taurus is also good at the sort of project management that gets the job done, and they are often good at detail, so editing print or film, with a reliable eye on the end product, can also find Taurus happily employed. A passion for cooking often finds them in a professional kitchen; or using their voice or their bodies, to sing, act or dance.

How Taurus chimes

From lovers to friends, when it comes to other signs, how does Taurus get along? Knowledge of other signs and how they interact can be helpful when negotiating relationships, revealed through an understanding of Sun sign characteristics that might chime or chafe. Understanding these through an astrological framework helps depersonalise potential frictions, taking the sting out of what appears to be in opposition, and can be really helpful. Harmonising relationships may have to be a learnt skill for dogmatic Taurus and this is partly dependent on what other planetary influences are at play in their personal birth chart, to temper or improve aspects of their Sun sign characteristics – especially those that can sometimes clash with other signs.

The Taurus woman

Strongly feminine, with Venus as her ruling planet, the Taurus woman values romance and passion. She has a keen eye for the real thing, but is unlikely to be swept off her feet, taking her time to diligently weighing up the pros and cons before committing. Generally good-natured, she can sometimes seem rather passive, but a deep confidence in her own talents, instincts and taste makes her very attractive.

NOTABLE TAURUS WOMEN

The elegance of Taurus is easily seen in actresses Audrey Hepburn and Cate Blanchett, while ballet dancer Darcey Bussell is grace and strength personified. Singers Barbra Streisand and Janet Jackson have the voice, and both Florence Nightingale and Queen Elizabeth II embody the strength, tenacity and dedication to duty that epitomises Taurus women.

The Taurus man

Although some of the words used to describe the Taurus man can make him seem rather stodgy, his trustworthy nature and passion are a winning and generally easy-going combination. He's someone who likes to take his time and savour his pleasures, giving his undivided attention for as long as his interest holds and generally when he's decided, he's in it – whatever it is – for the long haul.

Who love

Taurus & Aries

Taurus can benefit from a bit of Aries fire, and they both love the physical side of love, but arguments might arise from a clash in attitude towards money, so while an affair might work, a marriage could be tricky.

Taurus & Taurus

The downside of this like-minded union might be boredom because even though both will be hard-working and affectionate, they might be missing the initial spark that gets things off the ground.

Taurus & Gemini

Opposites attract and this earth/air combination could have wings, but probably only in the short-term, as Gemini's flighty attitude tends to clash badly with Taurus' more basic need for consistency and reliability.

Taurus & Cancer

The ease of this combination rests in their both having a commitment to the security of home, creating a lasting bond. Equally sensual, this combination bodes well for a harmonious sex life, too.

Taurus & Leo

Two big egos that are well matched in their physical appetites, sexually this earth/fire combination can work well, but there may be some tension between Taurus' reticence and Leo's need for extravagant gestures.

Taurus & Virgo

There's a deep bond waiting to happen between these well-matched earth signs, with their equal love of continuity and order. Virgo may find Taurus a tad physical, but can gain from a more passionate awakening.

Taurus & Scorpio

At first glance, there's not an obvious affiliation here but, in fact, both share a sexual bond that can make sparks fly. However, they are equally prone to streaks of possessiveness, which could cause friction.

Taurus & Libra

Both signs are ruled by Venus and have a mutual love of beauty and the finer things in life. While there's an airiness to Libra that lifts Taurean earthiness, the attraction of this may be short lived, becoming an irritation over time.

Taurus & Sagittarius

There's never a dull moment between these two signs that are naturally attracted to each other sexually, but Sagittarius' freewheeling attitude may chafe against the usual Taurus desire for a quieter, home-based existence.

Taurus & Aquarius

The highly innovative, cerebral aspects of this unconventional and airy sign tend to clash with the more down-to-earth approach of Taurus, making this combination generally too restrictive for Aquarius to last much beyond a fling.

Taurus & Pisces

Both sensualists, there may be a tad too much watery imagination for earthy Taurus, but there will be an appreciation of Pisces' creative side, and this balance can also play out well in the bedroom.

Taurus & Capricorn

Straightforward, physically complementary and sharing many similar goals, this combination may not be the most romantic but at its heart is an enduring friendship that is charmed by a well-matched sense of humour.

Taurus love-o-meter

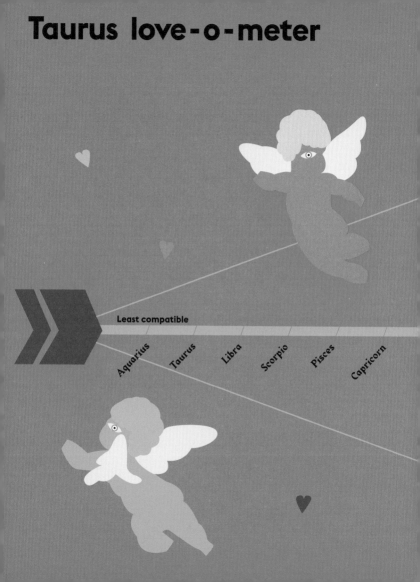

Least compatible

Aquarius · Taurus · Libra · Scorpio · Pisces · Capricorn

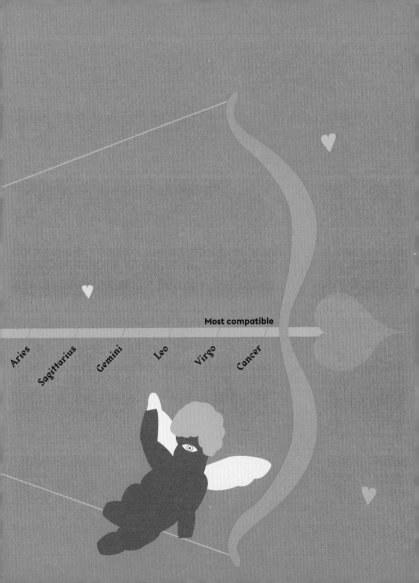

Most compatible

Aries Sagittarius Gemini Leo Virgo Cancer

The Taurus

II.

Deep Dive

In this section, dive deeper into the ways in which your Sun sign might be driving you or holding you back, and start to think about how you might use this knowledge to inform your path.

The
Taurus
home

The first thing that probably strikes others about a Taurus home is that it's tidy. It may have many beautiful *objets d'art* and pictures on the wall, but the rugs will be straight, the books neatly on the shelves, and the bed made. When Taurus comes home from a hard day at work, it needs to feel like a calm sanctuary with everything in its place. The kitchen, in particular, is often a give-away to Taurus' priorities: it's likely to be well stocked with gleaming copper pans, with a modern cooker and food processor.

There are often lovely textures in the fabrics and furnishings, set against beautiful wooden parquet or flagged stone floors. Colours are likely to be on the earthy spectrum, including greens, russets and browns and there may also be some very fine and well-tended houseplants.

For many Taureans, their love of nature and their natural green fingers can mean that their gardens are an extension of their home, or there may be a conservatory, greenhouse, patio or roof terrace, because being in touch with the soil in one way or another suits their need to feel grounded.

TOP TIPS FOR TAURUS' SELF-CARE

★ Take care of that throat, and keep chills at bay with a green scarf.

★ Alternate that rather basic, floor-based exercise routine with some aerobics.

★ Balance those gourmet dishes with some plainer, less calorific fare.

Self-care

Taurus is one of the few astrological signs that doesn't
need convincing that self-care is important: they practically
invented it. They aren't particularly neurotic, so their sleep
is usually undisturbed by worry. Too rational to be much of
a hypochondriac, minor aches and pains won't concern them
much. This calm, rather bovine demeanour does not, however,
mean they don't take self-care seriously – they do, and they
are probably quite a regular at the local yoga class.

Because of their love of routine, once they have an exercise
schedule they're likely to stick to it. In fact, the Taurus idea
of bliss is a regular visit to a health and beauty sanctuary where
they can do a bit of exercise and then a lot of chilling out on
the massage table or in the sauna. In the same spirit, their
bathroom is probably something of a sanctuary, too, with lots
of lovely lotions and soft, fluffy towels. It's all about the sensual
experience and this is what makes Taurus happy after toiling
away at the work place. There can be a slight vanity to Taurus'
self-care routine that is unsurprising since, being ruled by
Venus, beauty is highly prized.

WHAT TO KEEP IN THE TAURUS PANTRY

* Bouquet garni – probably created from their own home-grown herbs.

* Authentic 80% cocoa chocolate bar for cooking with.

* First pressed virgin olive oil.

Food
and
cooking

For a sensualist like Taurus, it's not just the taste of the food that matters, but also its look, smell and texture. A plate of food isn't just fuel, it has the potential to be a work of art. They may like their recipes tried and tested, but Taurus isn't averse to embellishment, improving taste or look, or just going a bit over the top in their cake decoration.

Taurus knows the value of first-class ingredients, too, and would prefer to cook a delicacy like *coq au vin* than chicken casserole, even though the rest of us might think it's the same thing. Taurus also enjoys the process of cooking: the meditative chopping and slicing and stirring. Even after a long day at work, a simple mushroom risotto, authentically made, is more their style than a boiled egg eaten on the go. For the bull, it's as much about the pleasure of the process as the actual eating.

TOP TIPS FOR
TAURUS' MONEY

★ Keep your money safe, but
  somewhere other than under
  the bed.

★ In between grafting to earn,
  remember to take the time
  to enjoy it.

★ Rational choices about saving
  will always be your first choice.

How Taurus handles money

Taurus understands money like no other astrological sign: they know its value, how to earn it, how to save it, how to invest it and how to spend it. There's no luck involved with how they accumulate wealth though, it comes down to hard work. And this can include astutely working the financial markets and researching carefully before they invest. You won't find them buying Bitcoins or gambling at the casino, that's not their style and it's too risky for Taurus. When it comes to handling money, it has to exist in the here and now, bricks and mortar, if necessary, not in some virtual currency.

There's nothing profligate in Taurus' nature. A bull market is a financial term for a market where share prices are rising and provoking acquisition and Taurus is all about taking possession of value. For Taurus, money represents security so they will always want to have a decent stash for a rainy day and a good retirement pension. The only downside with Taurus and money is that, generally, they would prefer to spend on themselves than others so can sometimes appear a little mean when it comes to buying gifts.

How Taurus handles the boss

Taurus often looks to the workplace for security and peace of mind and can sometimes look specifically towards a boss to provide this. This can occasionally make them rather compliant and, depending on what area or industry they work in, can be tricky if they are required to show a more independent mind, initiative or innovation.

A natural team player, Taurus' hard work often inspires others, making them generally a popular employee. Taurus' ability to listen and offer some well-considered feedback is something else the team is likely to appreciate, as their instincts are usually well grounded and clearly thought through before being offered. Fellow workmates appreciate their positive disposition: they are not a gossip, like a joke, dislike office dramas and seldom provoke them.

What the boss also values in a Taurus employee is their tenacity and ability to stick with a task and deliver it to the best of their ability, and when it comes to delegation, there's no one better to trust than a Taurus employee. They can make this work to their advantage, too, because hard graft and conscientious application can lead to promotion.

TOP TIPS TO
HANDLE THE BOSS

✳ Use your natural humour and empathy to progress an idea.

✳ Be sure to agree a plan, rather than steam ahead in the way you think best.

✳ Remind your boss that you're not slow, just careful, and the results speak for themselves.

TOP TIPS FOR
AN EASIER LIFE

★ Try not to get mad when
  the dishwasher isn't stacked
  exactly as you'd like.

★ Have a rota for domestic
  chores by all means, but be
  open to flexibility.

★ If you hate having to share
  possessions, keep your most
  prized things locked away.

What is Taurus like to live with?

A desire for beautiful surroundings alongside a practical streak means that daily chores get done, the bathroom cabinet only contains what's needed and the washing up tends to be done every night, in an effort to create the calm, secure ambience that lies close to a Taurean heart. The Taurus home also tends to contain the best their budget can afford, whether it's sumptuous bath towels or a state-of-the-art kitchen spatula.

Taurus is considered one of the easier signs to live with, but only as long as things are going their way, which can require a bit of compromise as standing up to a bullish housemate can be tricky. Because Taurus has a love and appreciation of beautiful possessions, they can be very possessive, not necessarily great on sharing, and won't take kindly to having their stuff borrowed without permission (if at all!). But Taurus is known for their generosity in other ways, and they like their home to be comfortable and welcoming to guests, are hospitable and generous hosts, just as long as everyone remembers to wipe their feet on their way in.

How to handle a break-up

Break-ups are difficult for Taurus because they seldom commit unless they're 100 per cent sure and in it for the long haul. Any break-up is also hard because it presents a major change, and it may take Taurus a while to commit again having believed this one was 'the one'. If the break-up becomes acrimonious, Taurus can take this very badly, because it clashes with their basic need for harmony. Although capable of confrontation, even if they are the one to instigate a break-up, Taurus finds it hard to hurt the feelings of those they've once loved. Because of this they may not say much, which can make it difficult for their ex to understand why they're breaking up in the first place.

TOP TIPS FOR
AN EASIER BREAK-UP

* Be very clear about how you feel, rather than veering away from the issue.

* If it comes as a surprise, press pause before reacting, because change is always difficult.

* Try not to argue over shared possessions; it's just not worth it.

How Taurus wants to be loved

Taurus wants to be loved often and well, with a lot of hugs in between. They like physical acknowledgement that they are cared for, so not for them the airy declarations of love – they want proof and that proof must lie in something tangible. This could be cooking a meal, which they'll appreciate because it's also how they like to show their love and appreciation. Or creating them something lovely for the home (as long as it reflects their taste), but it's not enough just to be told they're loved, Taurus will always seek evidence. The downside is that this can feel quite needy to more independent souls, but once reassured, Taurus is happy.

It's a bit of a conundrum, though, because their tendency to be reserved can make Taurus' own declarations of love few and far between. Despite this, still waters run deep and they are, more often than not, trustworthy friends and lovers. Extra-marital affairs aren't Taurus' style either, because their innate tendency to put down roots, combined with an element of laziness, makes them unlikely to stray. 'Why eat burgers out, when you can have steak at home?' might well have been said by a Taurus.

Because the throat is ruled by Taurus, many find their neck a particularly erogenous zone, and a neck and shoulder massage is sure to calm any stress that can arise from overwork. This sort of hands-on bodywork is, generally, a component of how Taurus wants to be loved. They are comfortable with their bodies and love to be massaged, preferably with essential oils in a beautiful location. It's a sure-fire way to calm a raging bull.

TOP TIPS FOR
LOVING TAURUS

* Cherish both body and soul: for Taurus they're very connected.

* Reliability is important to Taurus: once that date's in the diary, it's confirmed.

* It's not enough just to say 'I love you', there needs to be evidence.

Taurus' sex life

Because they are so much about the body, making love is first and foremost a physical connection for sensual Taurus and their foreplay tends towards the straightforward, with lots of eye contact. That physical connection is generally rooted in authenticity and trust, however, so is unlikely to be a one-night stand. Sex will probably have been anticipated and planned for in terms of a comfortable location, as Taurus is unlikely to be spontaneously overwhelmed by lust, which is just too unpredictable to feel comfortable. There can sometimes be an erotic delicacy to Taurean women, which also enhances their sensual style.

Once comfortable, Taurus can be playful, even earthy and bawdy in that Chaucerian way. As long as the trust is there, they are up for suggestions to explore new sexual territory and even role play, but only up to a point, as too much fantasy isn't a turn-on. What is really relished is that deep post-sex security: Taurus is very happy to sleep in another's arms. In fact, they often consider sex the best sleep aid there is.

Give

III.

Me & More

Your Sun sign never shows you the whole picture. In this section, learn how to read the nuances of your birth chart and discover a whole new level of astrological insight.

Your birth chart

Your birth chart is a snapshot of a particular moment, in a particular place, at the precise moment of your birth and is therefore completely individual to you. It's like a blueprint, a map, a statement of occurrence, spelling out possible traits and influences – but it isn't your destiny. It is just a symbolic tool to which you can refer, based on the position of the planets at the time of your birth. If you can't get to an astrologer, these days anyone can get their birth chart prepared in minutes online (see page 108 for a list of websites and apps that will do it for you). Even if you don't know your exact time of birth, just knowing the date and place of birth can create the beginnings of a useful template.

Remember, nothing is intrinsically good or bad in astrology and there is no explicit timing or forecasting: it's more a question of influences and how these might play out positively or negatively. And if we have some insight, and some tools with which to approach, see or interpret our circumstances and surroundings, this gives us something to work with.

When you are reading your birth chart, it's useful to first understand all the tools of astrology available to you; not only the astrological signs and what they represent, but also the 10 planets referred to in astrology and their individual characteristics, along with the 12 houses and what they mean. Individually, these tools of astrology are of passing interest, but when you start to see how they might sit in juxtaposition to each other, then the bigger picture becomes more accessible and we begin to gain insights that can be useful to us.

Broadly speaking, each of the planets suggests a different type of energy, the astrological signs propose the various ways in which that energy might be expressed, while the houses represent areas of experience in which this expression might operate.

Next to bring into the picture are the positions of the signs at four key points: the ascendant, or rising sign, and its opposite, the descendant; and the midheaven and its opposite, the IC, not to mention the different aspects created by congregations of signs and planets.

It is now possible to see how subtle the reading of a birth chart might be and how it is infinite in its variety, and highly specific to an individual. With this information, and a working understanding of the symbolic meaning and influences of the signs, planets and houses of your unique astrological profile, you can begin to use these tools to help with decision-making and other aspects of life.

Reading your chart

If you have your birth chart prepared, either by hand or via an online program, you will see a circle divided into 12 segments, with information clustered at various points indicating the position of each zodiac sign, in which segment it appears and at what degree. Irrespective of the features that are relevant to the individual, each chart follows the same pattern when it comes to interpretation.

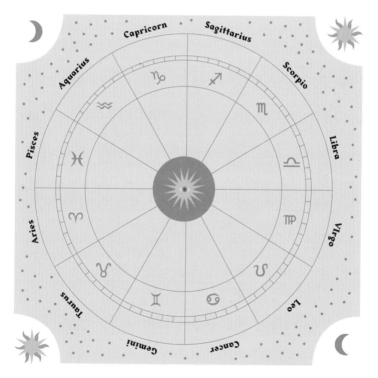

Taurus

Given the time of birth, the place of birth and the position of the planets at that moment, the birth chart, sometimes called a natal horoscope, is drawn up.

If you consider the chart as a clock face, the first house (see pages 95–99 for the astrological houses) begins at the 9, and it is from this point that, travelling anti-clockwise the chart is read from the first house, through the 12 segments of the chart to the twelfth.

The beginning point, the 9, is also the point at which the Sun rises on your life, giving you your ascendant, or rising sign, and opposite to this, at the 3 of the clock face, is your descendant sign. The midheaven point of your chart, the MC, is at 12, and its opposite, the IC, at 6 (see pages 101–102).

Understanding the significance of the characteristics of the astrological signs and the planets, their particular energies, their placements and their aspects to each other can be helpful in understanding ourselves and our relationships with others. In day-to-day life, too, the changing configuration of planets and their effects are much more easily understood with a basic knowledge of astrology, as are the recurring patterns that can sometimes strengthen and sometimes delay opportunities and possibilities. Working with, rather than against, these trends can make life more manageable and, in the last resort, more successful.

The Moon effect

If your Sun sign represents your consciousness, your life force and your individual will, then the Moon represents that side of your personality that you tend to keep rather secret or hidden. This is the realm of instinct, intuition, creativity and the unconscious, which can take you places emotionally that are sometimes hard to understand. This is what brings great subtlety and nuance to a person, way beyond just their Sun sign. So you may have your Sun in Taurus, and all that means, but this might be countered by an intuitive and mystical Moon in Pisces; or you may have your Sun in open-hearted Leo, but a Moon in Aquarius with all its rebellious, emotional detachment.

Phases of the Moon

The Moon orbits the Earth, taking roughly 28 days to do so. How much of the Moon we see is determined by how much of the Sun's light it reflects, giving us the impression that it waxes, or grows, and wanes. When the Moon is new, to us, only a sliver of it is illuminated. As it waxes, it reflects more light and moves from a crescent, to a waxing crescent to a first quarter; then it moves to a waxing gibbous Moon, to a full Moon. Then the Moon begins to wane through a waning gibbous, to a last quarter, and then the cycle begins again. All of this occurs over four weeks. When we have two full Moons in any one calendar month, the second is called a blue Moon.

Each month the Moon also moves through an astrological sign, as we know from our personal birth charts. This, too, will yield information – a Moon in Scorpio can have a very different effect to one in Capricorn – and depending on our personal charts, this can have a shifting influence each month. For example, if the Moon in your birth chart is in Virgo, then when the actual Moon moves into Virgo, this will have an additional influence. Read the characteristics of the signs for further information (see pages 12–17).

The Moon's cycle has an energetic effect, which we can see quite easily on the ocean tides. Astrologically, because the Moon is both a fertility symbol and attuned to our deeper psychological side, we can use this to focus more profoundly and creatively on aspects of life that are important to us.

Eclipses

Generally speaking, an eclipse covers up and prevents light being shed on a situation. Astrologically speaking, this will depend on where the Sun or Moon is positioned in relation to other planets at the time of an eclipse. So if a solar eclipse is in Gemini, there will be a Geminian influence or an influence on Geminis.

Hiding, or shedding, light on an area of our lives is an invitation to pay attention to it. Eclipses are generally about beginnings or endings, which is why our ancestors saw them as portents, important signs to be taken notice of. As it is possible to know when an eclipse is forthcoming, these are charted astronomically; consequently, their astrological significance can be assessed and acted upon ahead of time.

The 10 planets

For the purpose of astrology (but not for astronomy, because the Sun is really a star) we talk about 10 planets, and each astrological sign has a ruling planet, with Mercury, Venus and Mars each being assigned two. The characteristics of each planet describe those influences that can affect signs, all of which information feeds into the interpretation of a birth chart.

The Moon

This sign is an opposing principle to the Sun, forming a pair, and it represents the feminine, symbolising containment and receptivity, how we react most instinctively and with feeling.

Rules the sign of Cancer.

The Sun

The Sun represents the masculine, and is seen as the energy that sparks life, which suggests a paternal energy in our birth chart. It also symbolises our self or essential being, and our purpose.

Rules the sign of Leo.

Mercury

Mercury is the planet of communication and symbolises our urge to make sense of, understand and communicate our thoughts through words.

Rules the signs of Gemini and Virgo.

Venus

The planet of love is all about
attraction, connection and pleasure
and in a female chart it symbolises
her style of femininity, while in a male
chart it represents his ideal partner.

Rules the signs of Taurus and Libra.

Mars

This planet symbolises pure energy
(Mars was, after all, the god of War)
but it also tells you in which areas
you're most likely to be assertive,
aggressive or to take risks.

Rules the signs of Aries and Scorpio.

Saturn

Saturn is sometimes called the wise teacher or taskmaster of astrology, symbolising lessons learnt and limitations, showing us the value of determination, tenacity and resilience.

Rules the sign of Capricorn.

Jupiter

The planet Jupiter is the largest in our solar system and symbolises bounty and benevolence, all that is expansive and jovial. Like the sign it rules, it's also about moving away from the home on journeys and exploration.

Rules the sign of Sagittarius.

Uranus

This planet symbolises the unexpected, new ideas and innovation, and the urge to tear down the old and usher in the new. The downside can mark an inability to fit in and consequently be something of an outsider.

Rules the sign of Aquarius.

Pluto

Aligned to Hades (*Pluto* in Latin), the god of the underworld or death, the planet exerts a powerful force that lies below the surface and which, in its most negative form, can represent obsessions and compulsive behaviour.

Rules the sign of Scorpio.

Neptune

Linked to the sea, this is about what lies beneath, underwater and too deep to be seen clearly. Sensitive, intuitive and artistic, it also symbolises the capacity to love unconditionally, to forgive and forget.

Rules the sign of Pisces.

The four elements

Further divisions of the 12 astrological signs into the four elements of earth, fire, air and water yield other characteristics. This comes from ancient Greek medicine, where the body was considered to be made up of four bodily fluids or 'humours'. These four humours – blood, yellow bile, black bile and phlegm – corresponded to the four temperaments of sanguine, choleric, melancholic and phlegmatic, to the four seasons of the year, spring, summer, autumn, winter, and the four elements of air, fire, earth and water.

Related to astrology, these symbolic qualities cast further light on characteristics of the different signs. Carl Jung also used them in his psychology, and we still refer to people as earthy, fiery, airy or wet in their approach to life, while sometimes describing people as 'being in their element'. In astrology, those Sun signs that share the same element are said to have an affinity, or an understanding, with each other.

Like all aspects of astrology, there is always a positive and a negative, and a knowledge of any 'shadow side' can be helpful in terms of self-knowledge and what we may need to enhance or balance out, particularly in our dealings with others.

Air

GEMINI ✱ LIBRA ✱ AQUARIUS

The realm of ideas is where these air signs excel. Perceptive and visionary and able to see the big picture, there is a very reflective quality to air signs that helps to vent situations. Too much air, however, can dissipate intentions, so Gemini might be indecisive, Libra has a tendency to sit on the fence, while Aquarius can be very disengaged.

Fire

ARIES ✱ LEO ✱ SAGITTARIUS

There is a warmth and energy to these signs, a positive approach, spontaneity and enthusiasm that can be inspiring and very motivational to others. The downside is that Aries has a tendency to rush in headfirst, Leo can have a need for attention and Sagittarius can tend to talk it up but not deliver.

Earth

TAURUS ✶ VIRGO ✶ CAPRICORN

Characteristically, these signs enjoy sensual pleasure, enjoying food and other physical pleasures, and they like to feel grounded, preferring to base their ideas in facts. The downside is that Taureans can be stubborn, Virgos can be pernickety and Capricorns can veer towards a dogged conservatism.

Water

CANCER ✶ SCORPIO ✶ PISCES

Water signs are very responsive, like the tide ebbing and flowing, and can be very perceptive and intuitive, sometimes uncannily so because of their ability to feel. The downside is – watery enough – a tendency to feel swamped, and then Cancer can be both tenacious and self-protective, Pisces chameleon-like in their attention and Scorpio unpredictable and intense.

Cardinal, fixed and mutable signs

In addition to the 12 signs being divided into four elements, they can also be grouped into three different ways in which their energies may act or react, giving further depth to each sign's particular characteristics.

Cardinal

ARIES ✳ CANCER ✳ LIBRA ✳ CAPRICORN

These are action planets, with an energy that takes the initiative and gets things started. Aries has the vision, Cancer the feelings, Libra the contacts and Capricorn the strategy.

Fixed

TAURUS ✳ LEO ✳ SCORPIO ✳ AQUARIUS

Slower but more determined, these signs work to progress and maintain those initiatives that the cardinal signs have fired up. Taurus offers physical comfort, Leo loyalty, Scorpio emotional support and Aquarius sound advice. You can count on fixed signs, but they tend to resist change.

Mutable

GEMINI ✳ VIRGO ✳ SAGITTARIUS ✳ PISCES

Adaptable and responsive to new ideas, places and people, mutable signs have a unique ability to adjust to their surroundings. Gemini is mentally agile, Virgo is practical and versatile, Sagittarius visualises possibilities and Pisces is responsive to change.

The 12 houses

The birth chart is divided into 12 houses, which represent separate areas and functions of your life. When you are told you have something in a specific house – for example, Libra (balance) in the fifth house (creativity and sex) – it creates a way of interpreting the influences that can arise and are particular to how you might approach an aspect of your life.

Each house relates to a Sun sign, and in this way each is represented by some of the characteristics of that sign, which is said to be its natural ruler.

Three of these houses are considered to be mystical, relating to our interior, psychic world: the fourth (home), eighth (death and regeneration) and twelfth (secrets).

1st House

THE SELF

RULED BY ARIES

This house symbolises the self: you, who you are and how you represent yourself, your likes, dislikes and approach to life. It also represents how you see yourself and what you want in life.

2nd House

POSSESSIONS

RULED BY TAURUS

The second house symbolises your possessions, what you own, including money; how you earn or acquire your income; and your material security and the physical things you take with you as you move through life.

3rd House

COMMUNICATION

RULED BY GEMINI

This house is about communication and mental attitude, primarily how you express yourself. It's also about how you function within your family, and how you travel to school or work, and includes how you think, speak, write and learn.

4th House

HOME

RULED BY CANCER

This house is about your roots and your home or homes, present, past and future, so it includes both your childhood and current domestic set-up. It's also about what home and security represent to you.

5th House

CREATIVITY

RULED BY LEO

Billed as the house of creativity and play, this also includes sex, and relates to the creative urge, the libido, in all its manifestations. It's also about speculation in finance and love, games, fun and affection: affairs of the heart.

6th House

HEALTH

RULED BY VIRGO

This house is related to health: our own physical and emotional health, and how robust it is; but also those we care for, look after or provide support to – from family members to work colleagues.

7th House

PARTNERSHIPS

RULED BY LIBRA

The opposite of the first house, this reflects shared goals and intimate partnerships, our choice of life partner and how successful our relationships might be. It also reflects partnerships and adversaries in our professional world.

8th House

REGENERATION

RULED BY SCORPIO

For death, read regeneration or spiritual transformation: this house also reflects legacies and what you inherit after death, in personality traits or materially. And because regeneration requires sex, it's also about sex and sexual emotions.

9th House

TRAVEL

RULED BY SAGITTARIUS

The house of long-distance travel and exploration, this is also about the broadening of the mind that travel can bring, and how that might express itself. It also reflects the sending out of ideas, which can come about from literary effort or publication.

11th House

FRIENDSHIPS

RULED BY AQUARIUS

The eleventh house is about friendship groups and acquaintances, vision and ideas, and is less about immediate gratification but more concerning longer-term dreams and how these might be realised through our ability to work harmoniously with others.

12th House

SECRETS

RULED BY PISCES

Considered the most spiritual house, it is also the house of the unconscious, of secrets and of what might lie hidden, the metaphorical skeleton in the closet. It also reflects the secret ways we might self-sabotage or imprison our own efforts by not exploring them.

10th House

ASPIRATIONS

RULED BY CAPRICORN

This represents our aspiration and status, how we'd like to be elevated in public standing (or not), our ambitions, image and what we'd like to attain in life, through our own efforts.

The ascendant

Otherwise known as your rising sign, this is the sign of the zodiac that appears at the horizon as dawn breaks on the day of your birth, depending on your location in the world and time of birth. This is why knowing your time of birth is a useful factor in astrology, because your 'rising sign' yields a lot of information about those aspects of your character that are more on show, how you present yourself and how you are seen by others. So, even if you are a Sun Taurus, but have Sagittarius rising, you may be seen as someone who is freewheeling, with a noticeable taste for adventure in one way or another. Knowing your own ascendant – or that of another person – will often help explain why there doesn't seem to be such a direct correlation between their personality and their Sun sign.

As long as you know your time of birth and where you were born, working out your ascendant using an online tool or app is very easy (see page 108). Just ask your mum or other family members, or check your birth certificate (in those countries that include a birth time). If the astrological chart were a clock face, the ascendant would be at the 9 o'clock position.

The descendant

The descendant gives an indication of a possible life partner, based on the idea that opposites attract. Once you know your ascendant, the descendant is easy to work out as it is always six signs away: for example, if your ascendant is Virgo, your descendant is Pisces. If the astrological chart were a clock face, the descendant would be at the 3 o'clock position.

The midheaven (MC)

Also included in the birth chart is the position of the midheaven or MC (from the Latin, *medium coeli*, meaning middle of the heavens), which indicates your attitude towards your work, career and professional standing. If the astrological chart were a clock face, the MC would be at the 12 o'clock position.

The IC

Finally, your IC (from the Latin, *imum coeli*, meaning the lowest part of the heavens) indicates your attitude towards your home and family, and is also related to the end of your life. Your IC will be directly opposite your MC: for example, if your MC is Aquarius, your IC is Leo. If the astrological chart were a clock face, the IC would be at the 6 o'clock position.

Saturn return

Saturn is one of the slower-moving planets, taking around 28 years to complete its orbit around the Sun and return to the place it occupied at the time of your birth. This return can last between two to three years and be very noticeable in the period coming up to our thirtieth and sixtieth birthdays, often considered to be significant 'milestone' birthdays.

Because the energy of Saturn is sometimes experienced as demanding, this isn't always an easy period of life. A wise teacher or a hard taskmaster, some consider the Saturn effect as 'cruel to be kind' in the way that many good teachers can be, keeping us on track like a rigorous personal trainer.

Everyone experiences their Saturn return relevant to their circumstances, but it is a good time to take stock, let go of the stuff in your life that no longer serves you and revise your expectations, while being unapologetic about what you would like to include more of in your life. So if you are experiencing or anticipating this life event, embrace and work with it because what you learn now – about yourself, mainly – is worth knowing, however turbulent it might be, and can pay dividends in how you manage the next 28 years!

Mercury retrograde

Even those with little interest in astrology often take notice when the planet Mercury is retrograde. Astrologically, retrogrades are periods when planets are stationary but, as we continue to move forwards, Mercury 'appears' to move backwards. There is a shadow period either side of a retrograde period, when it could be said to be slowing down or speeding up, which can also be a little turbulent. Generally speaking, the advice is not to make any important moves related to communication on a retrograde and, even if a decision is made, know that it's likely to change.

Given that Mercury is the planet of communication, you can immediately see why there are concerns about its retrograde status and its link to communication failures – of the old-fashioned sort when the post office loses a letter, or the more modern technological variety when your computer crashes

– causing problems. Mercury retrograde can also affect travel, with delays in flights or train times, traffic jams or collisions. Mercury also influences personal communications: listening, speaking, being heard (or not), and can cause confusion or arguments. It can also affect more formal agreements, like contracts between buyer and seller.

These retrograde periods occur three to four times a year, lasting for roughly three weeks, with a shadow period either side. The dates in which it happens also mean it occurs within a specific astrological sign. If, for example, it occurs between 25 October and 15 November, its effect would be linked to the characteristics of Scorpio. In addition, those Sun sign Scorpios, or those with Scorpio in significant placements in their chart, may also experience a greater effect.

Mercury retrograde dates are easy to find from an astrological table, or ephemeris, and online. These can be used in order to avoid planning events that might be affected around these times. How Mercury retrograde may affect you more personally requires knowledge of your birth chart and an understanding of its more specific combination of influences with the signs and planets in your chart.

If you are going to weather a Mercury retrograde more easily, be aware that glitches can occur so, to some extent, expect delays and double-check details. Stay positive if postponements occur and consider this period an opportunity to slow down, review or reconsider ideas in your business or your personal life. Use the time to correct mistakes or reshape plans, preparing for when any stuck energy can shift and you can move forward again more smoothly.

Further reading

Astrology Decoded (2013)
by Sue Merlyn Farebrother;
published by Rider

Astrology for Dummies
(2007) by Rae Orion;
published by Wiley Publishing

*Chart Interpretation
Handbook: Guidelines for
Understanding the Essentials
of the Birth Chart* (1990)
by Stephen Arroyo;
published by CRCS
Publications

Jung's Studies in Astrology
(2018) by Liz Greene;
published by RKP

*The Only Astrology
Book You'll Ever Need*
(2012) by Joanne Woolfolk;
published by Taylor Trade

Websites

astro.com

astrologyzone.com

jessicaadams.com

shelleyvonstrunkel.com

Apps

Astrostyle

Co-Star

Susan Miller's Astrology Zone

The Daily Horoscope

The Pattern

Time Passages

Acknowledgements

Particular thanks are due to my trusty team of Taureans. Firstly, to Kate Pollard, Publishing Director at Hardie Grant, for her passion for beautiful books and for commissioning this series. And to Bex Fitzsimons for all her good natured and conscientious editing. And finally to Evi O. Studio, whose illustration and design talents have produced small works of art. With such a star-studded team, these books can only shine and for that, my thanks.